Big

Science Ideas

What is an Omnivore?

Bobbie Kalman

🌱 **Crabtree Publishing Company**

www.crabtreebooks.com

Big Science Ideas

Created by Bobbie Kalman

FSC
Mixed Sources
Cert no. SW-COC-001271
© 1996 FSC

Dedicated by Kylan Mitchell
To Wendy Mitchell, who taught me everything that is important in life, and how to persevere against all odds to protect what's worth living for. I love you, mom.

Author and Editor-in-Chief
Bobbie Kalman

Editors
Reagan Miller
Robin Johnson

Photo research
Crystal Sikkens

Design
Bobbie Kalman
Katherine Kantor
Samantha Crabtree (cover)

Production coordinator
Katherine Kantor

Illustrations
Bonna Rouse: page 11

Photographs
© BigStockPhoto.com: pages 21 (bottom), 27 (bottom), 28 (top)
© Dreamstime.com: pages 5 (bottom), 8 (bottom), 11, 17 (bottom), 19 (bottom)
© iStockphoto.com: pages 1, 5 (top), 9 (bottom), 20 (top), 25, 26 (top)
© ShutterStock.com: front cover, pages 3, 4, 6, 7, 9 (top), 10, 13, 14 (bottom), 15, 18, 19 (top), 20 (bottom), 21 (top), 23, 26 (bottom), 28 (bottom), 30, 31 (bottom)
Other images by Comstock, Corel, Creatas, Digital Stock, Digital Vision, and Otto Rogge Photography

Library and Archives Canada Cataloguing in Publication

Kalman, Bobbie, 1947-
    What is an omnivore? / Bobbie Kalman.

(Big science ideas)
Includes index.
ISBN 978-0-7787-3276-1 (bound)
ISBN 978-0-7787-3296-9 (pbk.)

1. Omnivores--Juvenile literature. I. Title. II. Series.

QL756.5.K35 2007   j591.5'3   C2007-904231-7

Library of Congress Cataloging-in-Publication Data

Kalman, Bobbie.
    What is an omnivore? / Bobbie Kalman.
       p. cm. -- (Big science ideas)
    Includes index.
    ISBN-13: 978-0-7787-3276-1 (rlb)
    ISBN-10: 0-7787-3276-2 (rlb)
    ISBN-13: 978-0-7787-3296-9 (pb)
    ISBN-10: 0-7787-3296-7 (pb)
    1. Omnivores--Juvenile literature. I. Title. II. Series.

QL756.5K432 2007
591.5'3--dc22

                                            2007026961

Crabtree Publishing Company
www.crabtreebooks.com   1-800-387-7650

Published in Canada
Crabtree Publishing
616 Welland Ave.
St. Catharines, Ontario
L2M 5V6

Published in the United States
Crabtree Publishing
PMB16A
350 Fifth Ave., Suite 3308
New York, NY 10118

Published in the United Kingdom
Crabtree Publishing
White Cross Mills
High Town, Lancaster
LA1 4XS

Published in Australia
Crabtree Publishing
386 Mt. Alexander Rd.
Ascot Vale (Melbourne)
VIC 3032

Contents

What do they eat?

Animals are living things. All living things need food to survive. Food gives living things the **energy** to grow and move. Animals eat different kinds of foods. Some animals eat mainly plants. Animals that eat mainly plants are called **herbivores**. Some animals eat other animals. Animals that eat other animals are called **carnivores**.

The panda, shown above, is a herbivore. It eats mainly bamboo plants.
The lynx, shown right, is a wild cat. It is eating meat. All wild cats are carnivores.

Both kinds of food

Many animals eat both plants and other animals. These animals are called **omnivores**. Most people are omnivores, as well. The bodies of omnivores have **adapted**, or changed, so they can eat both kinds of foods.

What kinds of foods do you enjoy eating?

5

Eat what they find

Most omnivores are **opportunistic feeders**. Opportunistic feeders eat the foods that are available to them. They **scavenge**, or search, for any food they can find. Raccoons, foxes, bears, and many birds are opportunistic feeders.

Eating to live

Some carnivores, such as red foxes, have adapted to eating both plants and meat to survive. When they cannot find **prey**, or animals to hunt and eat, they eat plants. Animals that eat both kinds of food have better chances of staying alive.

Fed by people

Many animals that are raised by people have become omnivores because people feed them both kinds of foods. For example, dogs are carnivores, but most dog food also contains vegetables, which are plant foods.

Insect omnivores

Some of the smallest omnivores are insects. House flies are omnivores. They eat just about anything, including dead animals and rotting plants. They often **vomit**, or bring up, some of the food they have eaten. They vomit on top of the food they were eating. If you eat this food, you might get sick. House flies can carry **diseases**. Diseases make people sick.

Cockroaches

Cockroaches are also omnivores. They eat plant sap, dead animals and plants, and other foods they find. In people's homes, cockroaches can be dangerous. Like flies, these insects carry diseases.

Cockroaches eat foods they find and leave nasty germs behind.

Land and sea turtles

Turtles, snakes, and lizards belong to a group of animals called **reptiles**. Most reptiles are carnivores, but painted turtles are omnivores. Painted turtles eat insects, snails, frogs, and fish. They also eat plants such as these lily pads. Painted turtles live in ponds and lakes. They come out of the water to warm up in the sun.

Hawksbill sea turtles

There are eight **species**, or kinds, of sea turtles. Six of the eight species are carnivores. Green sea turtles are herbivores, and hawksbill sea turtles are omnivores. Hawksbill sea turtles eat sea grasses, but they also eat squids, fish, and sponges. These sea turtles have jaws shaped like beaks. The shape of their jaws helps them reach food between rocks and in other narrow places.

11

Bird omnivores

There are many kinds of gulls. People call these birds "sea gulls," but there is no gull by that name. The gulls below are common gulls. Common gulls are omnivores. They scavenge for food they can eat. They eat plant foods, as well as fish and insects. Gulls can be seen near restaurants. They eat the food that people throw away.

Blue jays

You can see blue jays at bird feeders. They eat seeds, but they eat other kinds of foods, too. Blue jays find food on the ground as well as in trees. They eat fruits, acorns, eggs, small birds, worms, and insects. They also eat food left by people, such as bread or meat.

blue jay

rhea

Rheas

Rheas are big birds that do not fly. They live in South America. Rheas are true omnivores. They like plant parts such as seeds, fruits, roots, and leaves, but they also eat insects, worms, and small lizards.

13

Mammal teeth

Carnivores have sharp canine teeth for piercing through skin.

Mammals are animals with some hair or fur. Most mammals have teeth to help them eat their food. Carnivores have four sharp, pointed teeth, called **canines**, at the front of their mouths. Canines help carnivores pierce skin and tear the **flesh**, or meat, of animals.

Herbivore teeth

This picture shows a horse's teeth. Horses are herbivores. The teeth of many herbivores are suited to the food they eat. A horse's **incisors**, or front teeth, help it bite through plants. A horse's back teeth, called **molars**, are for grinding plant foods such as grasses.

Both meat and plants

The teeth of many omnivores include incisors, canines, and molars. Incisors and canines are for biting, and molars are for chewing and grinding food. Some animals also have **premolars**. Premolars have two **cusps**, or ridges. They are between the canines and molars. Premolars do the work of both kinds of teeth.

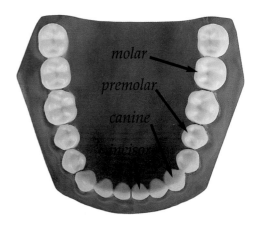

Count the incisors, canines, premolars and molars you have in your mouth. This picture shows a lower jaw.

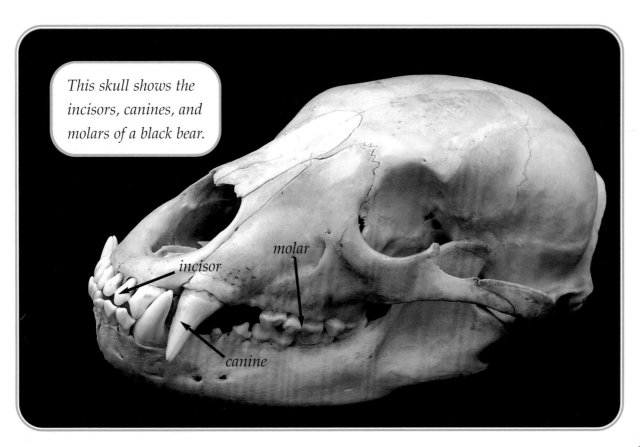

This skull shows the incisors, canines, and molars of a black bear.

15

Carnivore teeth

Red foxes have 42 very sharp teeth. They use their sharp teeth to grab prey. They swallow small animals whole. They tear bigger food apart and swallow the pieces. Red foxes are carnivores that live as omnivores. Even though red foxes have carnivore teeth, they have adapted their behavior to live as omnivores. Red foxes will eat almost anything to stay alive! They can even survive on a diet of fruit for several months.

Foxes have whiskers, just as cats do.

Hunting like cats

Foxes belong to the dog family, but they behave more like cats. They **stalk**, or follow, their prey the way cats do. Foxes slink along the ground and then **pounce**. To pounce is to jump high and come down on top of something, such as a mouse or rabbit.

Foxes eat all kinds of plant foods, such as fruits, leaves, and flowers. This fox is eating a daisy.

This red fox has seen a mouse. The mouse is hiding under the snow. The fox is now pouncing on the mouse.

Rodent omnivores

Rodents are small mammals with sharp front teeth that keep growing. Rodents must keep chewing to keep their front teeth short. Chipmunks are rodent omnivores. They eat seeds and nuts, but they also eat insects, bird eggs, and worms.

Chipmunks have large cheek pouches, where they can store a lot of food.

No rats are welcome!

Rats often eat the foods people grow, such as corn and wheat. They also eat insects, worms, and bird eggs. When they get into houses, rats will even chew electrical wires and cause fires! These rats are drinking milk in a barn.

This rat is munching on wood to keep its teeth from growing long.

Raccoon scavengers

Raccoons are omnivores that can find food anywhere. Many raccoons live in cities. They find food in parks, back yards, and even in people's homes. Raccoons have four sharp canine teeth for tearing meat. They eat plants, eggs, and small animals such as insects, fish, mice, and frogs.

This raccoon is eating an egg it found.

Raccoons are clever!

Raccoons once lived in forests. When people started cutting down forests, many animals lost their homes. Raccoons are clever and learned how to live near people and find food. Raccoons can even open doors and pry the lids off trash cans.

21

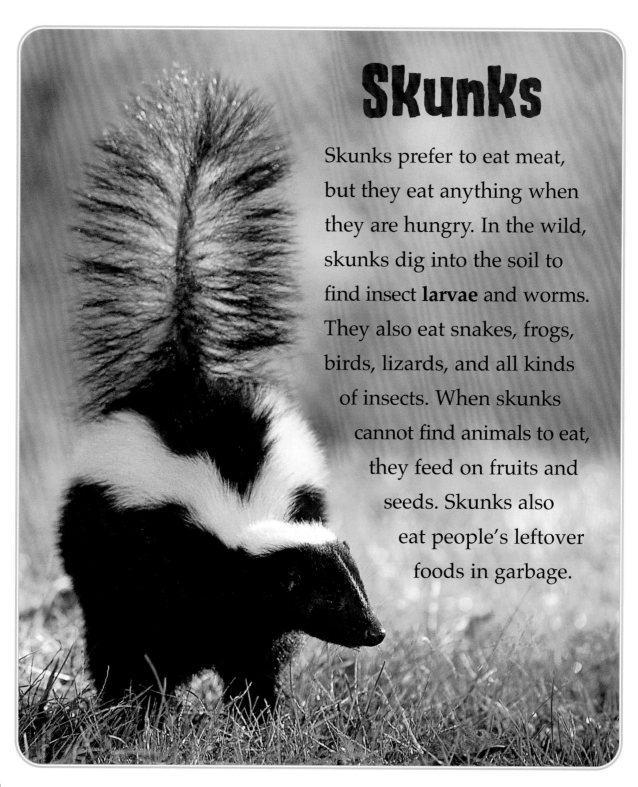

Skunks

Skunks prefer to eat meat, but they eat anything when they are hungry. In the wild, skunks dig into the soil to find insect **larvae** and worms. They also eat snakes, frogs, birds, lizards, and all kinds of insects. When skunks cannot find animals to eat, they feed on fruits and seeds. Skunks also eat people's leftover foods in garbage.

What is that smell?

People do not go near skunks, and most animals stay away, too. Skunks make a bad-smelling spray inside their bodies. This bear cub does not realize what will happen next! When a skunk stomps its feet and raises its tail, it is warning that it will spray. What do you think this bear cub will do when the skunk sprays it? What would you do?

23

Grizzly bears

Polar bears are carnivores, and pandas are herbivores, but most bears are omnivores. Brown bears, also called grizzlies, are omnivores. They eat nuts, berries, grasses, flowers, and roots. They eat honey, when they find a beehive. Not only do they eat honey, they eat the bees that made it, too. Grizzlies also eat animals such as rodents, deer, and even moose! They are scavengers, as well. They eat foods left behind by other animals or people.

It's salmon time!

Grizzlies are hunters and fishers. They have sharp claws for grabbing prey. When salmon swim in rivers, grizzlies stand in the water and grab them. Grizzlies use their sharp canine teeth for tearing apart the flesh of the salmon.

This grizzly cub has caught a salmon that was swimming in the river.

Opossum omnivores

Opossums live in trees or on the ground. They eat almost anything and keep moving from place to place to find food. Opossums eat fruits, insects, garbage, and dead animals. Opossums have 50 teeth. Most land mammals have fewer than 44 teeth.

Marsupial mammals

Opossums are mammals called **marsupials**. Most marsupials carry their babies in **pouches**, or pockets. Opossum mothers do not have full pouches. They have some folds of skin around their **teats**. The babies hang on to the teats and drink their mothers' milk.

Opossums can use their tails for grasping.

Virginia opossums are the only marsupials in North America.

27

Food for primates

You can see this mandrill's incisors and canine teeth.

Apes and monkeys belong to a group of animals called **primates**. People are primates, too. Most primates are omnivores. Their bodies are suited to eating both plants and animals. The monkey on the left is called a mandrill. Mandrills live in rain forests in Africa. They live on the ground and eat plants, insects, and small animals.

This squirrel monkey lives in a rain forest in South America. It lives up in the trees of the forest. This monkey eats fruits, nuts, eggs, and insects.

Chimp food

Chimpanzees are apes. They are omnivores. These smart apes are able to use tools to help them find food. The chimp above is using a stick to pull out insects from the ground. Chimps also eat fruits, nuts, seeds, roots, and grasses.

Look at these teeth! Are they like your teeth?

People omnivores

Most people are omnivores. We eat meat, fruits, and vegetables. We have the right teeth to eat meat as well as plant foods. Our bodies are also made to use the foods we eat. To stay healthy, however, we need to eat foods that are **nutritious**. Fruits, vegetables, eggs, milk, cheese, meat, and fish are great foods for humans!

Meat and veggies

This hamburger has meat, cheese, and mayonnaise, which come from animals. Mayonnaise is made from eggs. The burger also has tomato, lettuce, and bread. These foods come from plants. Bread is made from wheat. Wheat is a plant food.

Vegetarians are herbivores

Not all people are omnivores. Some people are **vegetarians**. Vegetarians do not eat any meat, but many vegetarians eat foods that came from animals, such as cheese and eggs.

These girls are making a vegetable pizza with cheese.

Glossary

Note: Some boldfaced words are defined where they appear in the book.

adapted Changed to become more suited to something

disease A sickness

energy The strength to use one's body; the power needed to move and grow

larvae Insects that have hatched from eggs; caterpillars and grubs are larvae

mammal An animal with hair or fur, which has a backbone, breathes air, and drinks its mother's milk as a baby

nutritious Describing food that helps the body grow and stay healthy

prey An animal that is hunted and eaten by another animal

primate A mammal that has hands, handlike feet, and eyes that face forward; monkeys, apes, and people are primates

reptile An animal with a backbone, cold blood, and scaly skin; alligators, crocodiles, lizards, snakes, and turtles are reptiles

scavenge To look for and collect anything that can be eaten

species Living things that are alike enough to make babies together

teat A body part on a mother mammal through which her baby sucks milk

Index

Printed in Canada — FR